ASD to Z...

Basic Information, Support, and Hope for

People Living with Autism Spectrum Disorders

Laurel A. Falvo

This booklet provides parents, grandparents, teachers, therapists, doctors, psychologists, employers, employees, children, adolescents, adults, and anyone who is interested with basic information about autism spectrum disorders (ASD) and available resources.

With thanks to the countless people who have taught and inspired me along the way, and to God, who gives me gifts, and opportunities to use them to bless others.

1

ASD to Z:

Basic Information, Support, and Hope for People Living with Autism Spectrum Disorders

ISBN: 978-1494932459
Copyright © 2005-2014 Laurel A Falvo

First Edition: November, 2005
Second Edition: June, 2008
Third Edition: November, 2011
Fourth Edition: January, 2014

Produced by Social Incites, LLC
www.socialincites.com

Holland, Michigan

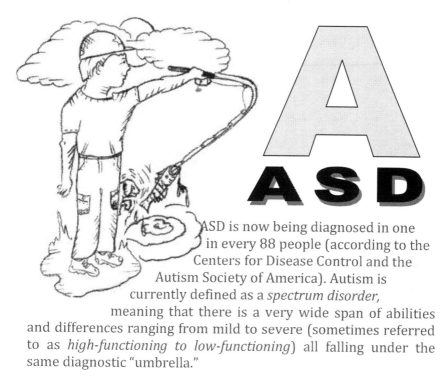

ASD is now being diagnosed in one in every 88 people (according to the Centers for Disease Control and the Autism Society of America). Autism is currently defined as a *spectrum disorder*, meaning that there is a very wide span of abilities and differences ranging from mild to severe (sometimes referred to as *high-functioning to low-functioning*) all falling under the same diagnostic "umbrella."

Individuals with ASD may have one of a variety of diagnoses. The diagnosis given may depend on the professional performing the evaluation and his/her training, area of specialization, past exposure to people with the diagnosis, and perceptions of the autism spectrum. It will likely also be affected by the individual's current age and early development and/or delays, the level of functioning that the person displays, and his or her unique profile of strengths and challenges.

Common diagnoses or labels include: ASD, autistic-like, autistic tendencies, High-functioning Autism (HFA), PDD (Pervasive Developmental Disorder) and PDD-NOS (Pervasive Developmental Disorder-Not Otherwise Specified), and Asperger's Syndrome. (*Asperger's* is a term generally used for a subgroup of individuals at the high-functioning end of the autism spectrum. Its name comes from the Viennese pediatrician who first described it in the 1940's, Hans Asperger).

In addition to a diagnosis of ASD, a person may have co-morbid (co-occurring) conditions, including, but not limited to, ADHD (Attention Deficit Hyperactivity Disorder) or ADD, OCD (Obsessive Compulsive Disorder), Tourette's Syndrome (accompanied by tics), and mood and anxiety disorders.

Each person diagnosed with ASD is a unique individual. However, there are some "typical" characteristics of ASD that are outlined in this booklet. It is important to note that not all individuals with autistic tendencies receive a formal diagnosis, yet many benefit from some of the same interventions.

The fact that you are reading this booklet likely means that there is someone in your life (maybe even yourself) who has been diagnosed—or may soon be diagnosed—on the autism spectrum. You are a very important part of the "social equation." Even though ASD is often regarded as a "social disability" because so many of the characteristics have social implications, it takes more than one person to engage in a social interaction. The success of those interactions is based primarily on three things:

    1. Individuals with ASD need relevant information about themselves and their social environment;

    2. Those who interact with them need to celebrate their strengths and understand their challenges;

    3. Everyone needs to understand his or her role in each social interaction, and respond effectively.

Much can be done to enable people with ASD to be successful, beginning with education, understanding, flexibility, and compassion. In keeping with the mission of SOCIAL INCITES, LLC, this publication seeks to help all individuals grow personally and interpersonally. We hope that you will utilize this valuable tool and then pass it along to someone else who can benefit from it.

Many resources are available to better understand children, adolescents, and adults with ASD, and to help them to be successful. More information about autism and related resource can be found at www.socialincites.com.

ASD is somewhat unique in that the diagnosis is made primarily by observing behaviors.

Many dictionary definitions focus on the end result when they define behavior. They employ terms such as, "observable activity, demeanor, manner," etc. Our common usage of the word "behavior" is generally consistent with these ideas. We tend to view others' actions as isolated, visible activities. If we assign any hint of prior action to it, we typically assign a choice. In other words, we often believe that people "choose" to "behave" a certain way. Of course, we're more likely to do this with negative behaviors than positive ones, especially with a person who frequently "misbehaves!" Perhaps the most insightful information is from the American Heritage Dictionary, which states, after giving synonyms for behavior, "These nouns all pertain to a person's actions as they constitute a means of evaluation by others." Note that "behavior" as defined in this way, depends very much on the person doing the observing!

Buried in some of the definitions of "behavior" is the word "reaction." What this implies is that there's an antecedent for the behavior; that the observable action is in response to something else. In fact, whether or not an action was based on a conscious choice, a "behavior" is usually a *response* to input.

Behaviors are the "B" in the ABC's of relationships. The necessary "bookends" are *antecedents* and *consequences.* When evaluating behaviors, we need to first look at the antecedents—the causes, or the environment or situation that is present when the behaviors occur. Often some detective work (particularly evaluating when, where, and how often the behavior occurs, in what social context, and following or accompanying which triggers) enables us to understand why a behavior is occurring, and perhaps how it can be avoided. We also need to evaluate the consequences that a person is experiencing along with the behavior. If there are no negative consequences, it may not be surprising to find that the behavior continues. If the consequence is that the person receives much-needed attention, whether the attention is positive or negative, the person may continue the behavior as the attention unwittingly reinforces it. Often the most effective consequences are "natural" consequences; those which are closely tied with the behavior.

Knowledge about autism spectrum disorders, and of the individual with ASD, can lead to an understanding of the various behaviors exhibited. Frequently, the cause of negative behaviors is related to anxiety, sensory over or under-stimulation, and/or a lack of understanding of social interactions and expectations of others. It is important to abandon all assumptions, and to take time to get to the root of the issue, not simply blaming the individual or the diagnosis, but helping to uncover the underlying reason for the behavior.

Generally behaviors serve a purpose, and may be communicating an important need! Yet it is also crucial that individuals with ASD learn to produce responses that work with other people, or that are *socially effective.* The ability to be socially effective is a basic component of everyday success!

COMPREHENSION and CONTEXT

Even though some have quite extensive and/or advanced vocabularies, most people with ASD frequently experience difficulty with comprehension.

This challenge occurs not only with spoken or written language, but also with "social" language, including difficulty "reading" body language, unspoken social rules, intent, and facial expressions, and making accurate guesses about the thoughts of others.

Obviously, people differ from one another in their ability to adequately "read" and respond effectively to the social context, or the people around them. One hallmark of autism spectrum disorders is that people with ASD struggle with this. Their challenges in the areas of executive functioning, theory of mind, emotional/social intelligence, boundary intelligence, gestalt processing, etc. create gaps in their ability to make necessary connections with others and experience social success. But they are not the only ones who experience challenges and gaps in these areas! Although these "building blocks of social development" generally improve throughout our lives, different people develop them at different rates, and to different degrees. Our age, experiences, personality, abilities, preconceived ideas, sensory and other needs, and more, can all affect our understanding of the social context (and our connection to it) and our ability to produce socially effective responses.

One factor interfering with the ability of people with ASD to comprehend language in its various forms is their tendency toward literal interpretation. "While this may confuse those of us who use context or prior experience to impose a variety of meanings on language, it can also be a source of delightful humor, provided that everyone is in on the joke. For example, we may need to explain that there is no need to look for actual cats and dogs outside when it is raining very hard; instead, the saying 'it's raining cats and dogs' originated many years ago when animals took refuge on thatched roofs to stay warm, and lost their perch when the intense rains came." (Quote from *Insights on Autism and Asperger Syndrome,* by Laurel A. Falvo, available through www.socialincites.com).

A general rule of thumb when working with individuals with ASD is to "say what you mean, and mean what you say." Given their natural inclination to interpret things literally, use of sarcasm, puns, metaphors and idioms (where the literal interpretation of the words spoken may differ from the intended meaning) can cause confusion or significant miscommunication. Those who interact with people with ASD can help by limiting sarcasm and other "non-literal" uses of language. It is sometimes possible to gauge comprehension by asking the individual to rephrase what was said.

Taking time to listen to people with ASD may prove to be very enlightening, as we learn about our world through their unique way of comprehending life around them. And specific strategies (visuals, prompts, etc.) can be used to raise their awareness of others' expectations so that they can be successful in meeting those.

There is a popular saying, "You are what you eat."

Most people use this to refer to the fact that eating too much junk food makes it difficult for our body "engines" to function properly and efficiently. However, some people are affected even more dramatically by the food they eat!

Research has shown that there is a very close correlation between the functioning of the human brain and the food we consume. Often changes in physical, mental, and emotional functioning can be prompted by a change in diet. Keeping a food journal to note the possible relationship between positive and negative behaviors, emotions, and physical symptoms can be beneficial.

Many individuals with ASD are "picky" eaters. This may be due to sensory difficulties or preferences, poor muscle tone in the mouth (leading to difficulty with coordinated chewing and swallowing), health issues, or food intolerances or allergies. Often, autistic behaviors may be linked-- at least in part--to intolerance to proteins such as gluten and casein, to an overabundance of yeast, or to sensitivity to dyes or other food additives, or other common foods such as soy, eggs, and various fruit.

A team of qualified medical professionals can provide guidance in determining whether food allergies or intolerances may be contributing to a lack of or overabundance of energy, or difficulty

©2014 Laurel A. Falvo   9 making eye contact, skin rashes, intestinal distress, constipation or diarrhea, ear infections, language delays, chronic cough or runny nose, anxiety, or other physical, emotional, or mental difficulties.

Therapies, medications, and/or restricted or rotating diets can be utilized as appropriate to best meet the needs of individuals negatively affected by the food they eat. Although they can be intensive or expensive, "diets" to accommodate food allergies and intolerances are much more of a lifestyle change than a minor inconvenience, but the impact can be potentially life-altering.

Sometimes, when medical issues are ruled out as a primary factor, people are picky eaters because we allow them to be picky! We don't expect them to eat a variety of healthy foods, so they restrict themselves to familiar foods (or those that fall into a comfortable category they have created according to food group, color, texture, scent, etc.). Or we expect them to scream, or refuse to eat certain foods, and so they do! If this describes your situation, you are encouraged to find a "coach" to help you set healthy expectations and adhere to them even through the difficulties of breaking old habits and battling preconceived notions. Your coach may be a friend, colleague, family member, teacher or other professional, or perhaps a coach from Social Incites, LLC.

You may not know if a person is on a restricted diet. However, you can be sensitive to the fact that people have a variety of dietary needs. Parties and family gatherings provide numerous opportunities to try new, delicious foods. However, this may be upsetting to some individuals, or may create intestinal or behavioral problems for others when they eat unfamiliar or "trigger" foods. It is helpful to know that food will be involved in upcoming activities, so that suitable substitutes can be provided as needed. And food can be de-emphasized by putting focus on other types of activities and interests so that people are not tempted by foods they should not be eating, or do not feel left out when others are indulging in things they cannot eat.

A person's education should build on his or her strengths and address specific needs. For some, a specialized ASD placement is most appropriate. Others will benefit from *inclusion* (or "mainstreaming") - being in a regular classroom with any necessary supports. Some are successfully homeschooled. By far the best way to educate an individual with ASD is through a *team approach*, involving the student, parents, teachers, administrators, and any other professionals ("parapro" or aide, therapists, psychologist, social worker, etc.) who work with the student.

EDUCATION and EXPECTATIONS

Some students with ASD may need more supports than others, possibly including one or more of speech, occupational, physical, recreational, or cognitive behavioral therapies, supports on the playground, bus, and in the cafeteria, social skills groups, and peer mentoring. Others may need little or no specialized or individual supports.

It is important to note that an educational diagnosis is different from a medical diagnosis. Schools are typically required only to provide what is *educationally necessary*—or helps to develop the ability to learn and succeed in the classroom. Medical or more "physical" supports will need to be obtained outside of school. Many hospitals and other organizations provide private therapy and other treatment methods to help meet the needs of individuals with ASD.

An Individualized Education Plan (IEP) is formal paperwork that determines programming, taking into account the student's current level of performance, areas of difficulty, and measurable goals. The IEP is an important process, and a unique opportunity for parents and professionals to work together to promote learning and ensure a quality education for students with ASD.

It is crucial for parents, professionals, and peers to continue to *educate* themselves, both about ASD, and about the individuals affected by it. Self-awareness for the student with ASD is also crucial, aiding in the self-advocacy process required in higher education and other areas of adult life. This educational process can lead to informed decisions about the best educational, therapeutic, and other strategies to use in helping everyone to succeed in all areas of life.

Many of you are teaching in a classroom where there is an individual diagnosed with ASD. Would we teach differently if we knew that someone in the class had ASD, but we didn't know which one? Would we explain our directions more carefully? Would we work with the entire class to foster effective social interactions, rather than focusing on the directives of one student's IEP?

Many of you are parents of a child (or more than one child) with ASD. Would we parent differently if we accepted that our children--regardless of the presence of a diagnosis--need clear expectations, and predictable structure, including consistent, natural consequences for the choices they make? Do we parent one child differently because he or she has a diagnosis?

Clearly, the presence of ASD is an important consideration in teaching and parenting any given individual. Information about a diagnosis can help us better understand the perspective of the individual, and approach him or her with valuable strategies that may prove helpful in our parenting and teaching—and in their learning and interacting. But, we should ensure that we are working to know and appreciate each individual with whom we live and work, with or without a diagnosis, so that we can recognize and accommodate both their strengths as well as their challenges.

FRIENDS

What is friendship?

Most definitions of a "friend" focus on the recipient of affection and assistance. In other words, we tend to define our friends by what they do for us, or how they make us feel.

Is our tendency to view friendship in this manner consistent with our goal to promote social effectiveness?

What makes a good friend? Our list may include attributes such as honesty, affection, helpfulness, a willingness (and ability) to listen and compromise, shared interests, enjoyment of time spent together, etc. Frequently, parents and educators are concerned about whether individuals with ASD "have friends." Those with the diagnosis are often eager to have someone be a friend to them. Yet this may be one of the most difficult aspects of life for people with ASD. Contrary to popular belief, they do not necessarily choose to be alone. However, difficulty understanding social situations or initiating and maintaining effective connections, struggles with motor skills and motor planning, and misunderstandings on the part of the individual's peers often lead to ostracism and even bullying.

"The only way to have a friend is to be one."
(Ralph Waldo Emerson)

The truth is, we do not have control over what other people think, do, or say. When we make attempts at friendship, we do not know how they will be received. The only thing we have control over is our own thoughts, words, actions, and other responses. Focusing on BEING a friend, rather than "getting" or "making" friends, can make the world of friendship more open to genuine attempts.

"The best way to destroy an enemy is to make him a friend"
(Abraham Lincoln)

Many people, including those with ASD, have difficulty judging intent, or figuring out why people do what they do. This means that constructive criticism and helpful instruction can often be misinterpreted as bullying.

Daniel Goleman, who has researched "emotional intelligence" extensively, has developed a list of seven key abilities people need to effectively manage life:
- Motivating oneself
- Persisting against frustration
- Delaying gratification
- Regulating moods
- Holding onto hope
- Empathizing with others
- Controlling impulses

Mastery of traits in this list is integral to the eradication of bullying. People who have attained proficiency in these areas are more likely to treat others well. They also stand a lesser chance of becoming a target of bullying. And bystanders with these characteristics are more likely to intervene on someone else's behalf.

It is known that through an increased awareness of ASD and the use of specific techniques, individuals with autism can develop and maintain meaningful friendships and even marriage relationships. To encourage friendships, through modeling and direct instruction, we can teach our children how to exhibit friendly traits, rather than simply looking for them in others. We may find it to be contagious!

ASD to Z

When this booklet went to press, research had not yet determined one specific cause for ASD. However, research, combined with the fact that it is often diagnosed multiple times within families, confirms that in many cases there is a genetic link.

It is becoming increasingly common for a parent to pursue a personal diagnosis of ASD after his or her child is diagnosed. Someday we may discover multiple causes for ASD, and even numerous forms, or *subtypes* of the diagnosis, each possibly linked to different causes, and benefited by different treatments.

*There are often opportunities for individuals with ASD to participate in research studies as scientists strive to better understand the diagnosis.

Sometimes, the unexpected things in life invoke our sense of humor. They catch us off-guard, and make us laugh. Individuals with ASD frequently have a sense of humor, although the things that they find humorous might not be what others would anticipate. They are more likely to succeed in a wide variety of environments, including the classroom, when they are interacting with flexible individuals who possess a good sense of humor.

While our occasional unexpected responses may invoke others' sense of humor, they also have the potential to ostracize us. Fortunately, there are resources to help us navigate this fine line in order to help ourselves and others become more socially effective!

INTENSE INTERESTS

The interests of people with ASD may be either similar to or drastically different from those of their peers, and may change over time. But generally the special interests of an individual with ASD dominate their time and conversations. These intense areas of interest may include (but are not limited to): transportation, the solar system and other scientific areas, maps and schedules, video games, and other topics that lend themselves to predictability. A young child may indicate interest in parts of objects (doors or wheels on toy cars) rather than the whole, possibly spinning, tapping, or lining them up.

A person with ASD may need to be taught when and where it is appropriate to focus on his or her area of interest, but these interests may also be used to interact with others. They may even lead to a career as the individual gets older. Adults with ASD are often successful in fields involving mathematics, computers, and scientific research. It is speculated by many people that such famous historical figures as Ludwig van Beethoven, Wolfgang Amadeus Mozart, Vincent Van Gogh, Isaac Newton, Albert Einstein, and Lewis Carroll also displayed characteristics of the autism spectrum.

Our world has experienced and enjoyed many of the contributions of individuals with ASD in the area of restricted interests. Those intense interests, when channeled in ways that allow them to contribute to society, can provide personal employment and/or enjoyment to the individual, and sometimes great advances that benefit our communities and our world.

Temple Grandin is an individual with ASD who was encouraged to pursue and further develop her special interest in cattle. That has led to her extreme success in the meat-processing industry. In her writing she shares helpful strategies for using a person's talents and interests to be successful in contributing to our communities. She also provides valuable information for learning to meet the expectations of others in order to be socially successful. The movie of Temple Grandin's life (starring Claire Danes) is a great resource for better understanding the benefits of accommodating, encouraging, and appreciating people with ASD.

ASD to Z

JUGGLING

ABILITIES and CHALLENGES

Often our understanding of individuals with ASD is complicated by inconsistencies between their abilities and challenges. Some may have a low IQ or a form of a learning disability. Others may be gifted academically (either in all areas or just one or two specific areas). Some new information or skills may be learned quickly; others may take numerous attempts before they are learned. Compounding the confusion is the fact that the skills an individual appears to have may vary depending on the day or time of day, the social context, sensory environment, or other external factors. And strategies that work one day may not work every day.

Research results are implicating additional genes in the expression of autism spectrum disorders (ASD); genes which are not missing, but are prevented from turning on during the process of development. Perhaps most fascinating is the fact that the research "...strongly supports the emerging idea that autism stems from disruptions in the brain's ability to form new connections in response to experience – consistent with autism's onset during the first year of life, when many of these connections are normally made." *Harvard University, 2008.*

For those of you living or working with individuals with ASD, this is not news to you. It can be frustrating for caregivers as well as individuals on the autism spectrum that lessons learned from one experience often do not generalize to the next experience, leading parents and professionals to bemoan the fact that they have given certain instructions "one (or three) hundred times" or that "they should have learned this by now!"

So if the autistic brain doesn't readily support experience-dependent learning, what are we to do? Repeated exposure to activities and lessons may prove helpful, as the brain is given an opportunity to eventually form the connections that it needs. For example, if an individual has a weekly chore of taking out the trash on Fridays, after many weeks, months, or even years of doing so, he or she may eventually make the connection that because today is Friday, it is time to take out the trash. It may also be helpful to provide instruction which guides individuals through the process of making those connections and builds in meaning surrounding the activity. The individual can be taught (and prompted or reminded through visual cues, schedules, alarms, or other strategies) that the trash needs to be emptied and set out at the curb so that it can be taken away by the garbage truck which usually arrives on Friday. Providing social information (i.e. reasons for repetitive activities) may help the individual generalize to new experiences, not only remembering to put out the trash each Friday, but perhaps even being more accepting of a week which includes a holiday, requiring the trucks to be on the road collecting trash on Saturday instead of Friday!

It can be frustrating for a parent, grandparent, professional, or the individual with ASD to be faced with such a drastic disparity between talents/abilities and struggles/difficulties. However, the recipe for success will include a realistic look at the person's challenges, a pursuit of appropriate treatments, a celebration of his/her strengths, and opportunities to utilize talents and abilities in meaningful ways.

Individuals with ASD typically have a longer *learning curve*, and learn differently than *neurotypicals*, (individuals who do not have ASD). This means that parents, teachers, employers, and others working to help people with ASD succeed will need to provide multiple opportunities to learn and practice new skills, patiently trying a variety of strategies to find one or more that work well. Early intervention, and beginning to teach skills at a young age, gives people with ASD time to adjust to new expectations, and to learn the necessary strategies for being successful.

Until you've been a parent of a child with special needs, you cannot fully comprehend what it's like to worry about your child's future, to agonize over schooling and other decisions, and to celebrate ecstatically over each little milestone achieved. If you are not married to someone with autism or Asperger Syndrome, you may not adequately appreciate the potential difficulty getting your emotional needs met by someone who does not seem to sense or identify with those needs. Unless you've faced a classroom of eager (and sometimes impish) faces, you cannot truly grasp what it's like to have the strengths and challenges of each child resting in your hands for a school year, to be juggled with testing requirements, time constraints, and dwindling budgets

Everyone is capable of learning, whether to a lesser or greater degree, with the dedicated assistance of supportive people in their lives, combined with diligent work on the part of the individual.

NOTES: What have you learned since beginning your journey with autism? If you are living or working with a person with autism, what has he/she learned? What strategies have proven to be the most beneficial?

_____

_____

_____

_____

_____

_____

_____

There is an old saying, "Knowledge is Power." Demystifying the *social context*, by providing information about what people think, feel, know, believe, remember, expect, etc., can provide a level of control and comfort, and even success. It allows us to make *informed social choices.*

The field of psychology uses terms such as *Theory of Mind, Social IQ, Executive Functioning,* and *Emotional Intelligence* to describe components of a person's ability to understand oneself and others, and to respond effectively. Although these skills are not intuitive for many people, including those with ASD, there is much that can be done to provide valuable information that leads to successful interactions with others. A variety of resources and strategies can be utilized to raise awareness and specifically teach the following:

- How to identify and meet others' expectations;
- How to repair broken interactions;
- How to read body language, facial expressions, and other forms of nonverbal communication, and respond effectively;
- How to know what other people expect, and how to meet their expectations;
- How to develop and utilize healthy boundaries, defining and protecting each person's rights and responsibilities;
- How an individual's choices lead to positive or negative consequences, and what can be done to achieve desired outcomes;
- How to manage one's own emotions effectively and how to read others' emotions and respond appropriately.

Everyone benefits from knowledge of the individuals involved in a given social interaction, of the skills necessary for building and maintaining effective social connections, of autism spectrum disorders, and of available resources. This is the very foundation of social insight and effectiveness!

ASD to Z

Loss is frequently involved with a diagnosis of ASD. Parents and other family members may experience a feeling of loss, including the loss of dreams or a sense of direction for their lives, loss of support, and loss of social opportunities. Individuals with ASD may express behaviors and attitudes that are indicative of feelings of loss, including loss of routine, control, position, and friends.

Research varies when describing the different ways of responding to loss, grief, or change. But most indicate something similar to the following:

- *Denial:* Refusing to accept the change or the need for change;
- *Anger:* Often people will look for someone to blame, and may respond by lashing out at others—particularly those they choose to blame for the situation, but also anyone who may be close-by;
- *Bargaining:* Trying to find a way around the change, or trying to substitute other options for the proposed change;
- *Depression:* Sometimes people are so overwhelmed by change that it drags them down emotionally, and they find it difficult to function even in other areas;
- *Acceptance:* Accepting the change, and possibly even feeling empowered by it or enthusiastic about it.

Many people believe that the most important aspect of change is how we respond to it. Being flexible helps us adapt to loss or change. But loss and change can also lead to greater growth and success—if we let it!

MEMORY

Individuals with ASD may have an excellent memory for details, such as numbers, dates, statistics, unique facts, and information about areas of special interest. However, they may struggle with *working memory*, or remembering where they put their shoes, or when to turn in an assignment. Using visual cues, and providing plenty of prompts and *think time* as they retrieve information stored in their memory can help those with ASD be more successful in their social interactions.

There are strategies we can use to aid our working memory. Following are just a few:

- *Slow down.* Take time to think about what you are doing, to make note of important details (either mentally or by writing them down), and simplify your schedule where possible.

- *Take time to organize your time and materials.* While it may seem as though you do not have time to add extra steps to the process, you may actually end up saving time by organizing your drawers, cupboards, and computer bag so that everything has its place. Then take an extra minute to ensure that items are placed where they belong so that you can find them next time you need them. Using lists or a day-at-a-glance calendar can help organize time and tasks so that nothing is forgotten.

- *Take time to meet your other needs.* Your brain, just like the rest of your body, will function better when you are getting enough sleep and exercise, eating healthy foods, nurturing friendships, and occasionally spending time with a hobby or a good book.

- *Establish connections.* Have you just met someone new? Associate his or her name with someone else you know, or with a familiar object that will help you remember the name in the future. Use mnemonic devices to remember words, dates, or details. Organize your mental (or written) shopping list according to the sections in the store. Or develop a catchy tune to go with the information you need to remember. These social connections can be valuable in helping to improve your memory...or at least these people may be able to help you remember the things that need to be remembered!

Networking helps to ensure that everyone can access the best information and services in a most timely manner.

It also provides support and encouragement to those who need it.

Connecting with other people through networking is a great way to realize that you are not alone! Whether you are talking with or writing to people who can identify with your achievements and struggles, or accessing valuable resources to help with your particular situation, there are many benefits to networking in your community and around the world!

There are many parents and other family members, professionals, businesses, and organizations working to better understand and provide support for individuals with ASD. Often individuals with ASD are also working to advocate for themselves. Resources online and in your community are available to meet your needs. Numerous web sites, including www.socialincites.com and our Social Incites Facebook page are available to provide valuable information and support.

Often networking through social media sites is beneficial to individuals living with ASD. It is important to teach and model Internet safety to children, teens, and even adults with ASD, who may have difficulty judging others' intent, making decisions about what information to share and when, and how much time is reasonable to spend on the Internet. One of the resources available from Social Incites, LLC is a downloadable document, "Electronic Contracts," to provide more information and to help families be deliberate in teaching and enforcing healthy boundaries in this area.

The goal of networking is to connect people for the mutual benefit of everyone involved in the interaction!

MY NETWORKING: This page has been set aside for you to note the people, organizations, web sites, and other resources that are helpful for your personal journey:

_____

_____

_____

_____

_____

_____

_____

_____

_____

_____

_____

REMEMBER: YOU can also be a helpful resource for others!

Forging ahead with a task without planning the steps or considering the outcome can lead to unpleasant consequences. How often have you started a project without evaluating the time needed to complete it, the materials required, or the usefulness of the end result? Perhaps you are living with unfinished projects due to this issue, or have suffered the consequences of a job poorly done. Children who approach tasks in this way may end up being punished or having rewards taken away. Even adults may encounter a similar outcome in their workplace. Time and effort may be wasted as you restart the task to eliminate the results of beginning without planning. You may even miss opportunities for success due to your lack of planning.

organization

Over time, most of us learn to consider these lessons prior to beginning a task, which helps to protect us from frequent failure and unpleasant consequences, and may lead to greater productivity. Yet planning before work is often very difficult for those with ASD, even after repeated failures. Why is this?

One contributing problem may be difficulty with the concept of time. When a research paper is assigned in a high school class with a due date three weeks in the future, some students may write down the assignment and close their planners, unaware of the significance of the time allotted. When asked about their progress on the project, they may reply, "It's not due for three weeks!" The result for these students is that the due date comes and goes without a completed project, or the student picks up the task the night before the due date, thinking that the research paper can be completed in one night.

Lack of motivation may also be an issue. Often the hardest part of a task is getting started, and if the necessary motivation is missing, the job never gets started. Another common tendency for these students is to look ahead at the finished product, with no idea of the steps required to get there. A student may recognize the importance of the assignment and its due date, but be unable to define or sequence the steps needed to initiate the task and bring it to a successful completion.

Are these students doomed to a life of late assignments and "incompletes" on their report cards? Not at all! Sometimes they may need additional assistance from a teacher, parent, or tutor, with various deadlines spelled out for helping them to sequence and complete the tasks leading up to the final project. A checklist may prove helpful in these instances.

Understanding the different types of organization can empower parents and teachers to assist a person who has difficulty in this area. For example, there is a difference between *static organization*, which never changes (socks always go in the same drawer, recess is always at 10:00 a.m. on school days, etc.) and *dynamic organization* which involves a variety of changing variables (i.e. organizing a series of tasks in order to reach a goal or turn in an assignment).

Of course, being organized will not always protect us from regret, as some things will remain outside of our control. Think of the parties, programs, and other special events that you've spent hours planning, but which were affected by or succumbed to unexpected changes, weather-related disappointments, or other disruptions. We cannot guarantee success for those with ASD by teaching them to plan, but we know that when we're able to equip them with tools to deal with life as it comes, they are much more likely--as we are--to be successful. When we are equipped with tools for organizing our time and materials, we are all more likely to be successful!

PAspects of life, school, relationships, athletics, etc. may prove difficult for individuals with ASD. It is good that parents and teachers do what they can to insure the individual's ability to experience success. However, we should not want to make the path too easy, or remove opportunities for failure. To do so would be to cause them to miss out on opportunities to learn persistence and resilience. Instead, guided navigation of difficult tasks, and even failures, along with instruction which ensures that they learn valuable life lessons from these experiences, is the key to helping them develop both persistence and patience!

Persistence AND Patience

Sometimes we tend to be too quick to decide what other people cannot do, without giving them an opportunity to try something. It's well-documented that people with ASD may need more exposure to opportunities to learn new skills than their peers.. But often, if given the opportunity, they will exceed our expectations for their ability to succeed!

While we're at it, this might be a good time to consider the benefits that parents and professionals gain from opportunities to develop both persistence and patience! We may feel that we get abundant (and not always welcome) practice in both areas, but it likely serves us well!

How did you learn to do that? Do you need help?
Why did you tease your brother?
Didn't you know the assignment was due today?

It may be difficult for individuals with ASD to *answer questions*. Their ability to retrieve and share information stored in their memory may be limited by past experience, by the way a question is worded, and by whether the question can be answered accurately if interpreted literally. They might at times appear to have *selective hearing*, causing a parent or other person to wonder if they are paying attention, or are even able to hear. It may be that they simply need more time to process the  question, or need help modifying the sensory or social environment to decrease distractions, and increase their ability to focus and process information. They might need more information about what is expected, or about why a person is asking the question. They might be helped to respond more effectively through prompts, visual aids, and rephrasing of the request.

It may also be difficult for the individual to *ask questions*, either for information, or to gain help or assistance. Sometimes the person does not recognize that he/she needs assistance. *Auditory processing problems* can cause a person to hear something different than what is said, yet the individual most often does not realize that there is a discrepancy, even after others react negatively to their perceived lack of compliance. Individuals with ASD might not ask questions because they believe that doing so will display a lack of intelligence which will be judged negatively by others. When answering and asking questions does not come naturally, strategies can be helpful for explaining the concepts, and providing tools for interacting more effectively with others.

Since difficulties with answering questions can be a liability when dealing with law enforcement, it may be beneficial for an individual with ASD to carry a card or other identifying item disclosing his/her diagnosis, and providing other emergency contacts who may be able to help clear up any confusion. (One is available through Social Incites, LLC).

ASD to Z

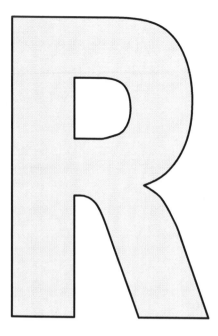

Individuals with ASD typically crave routine and predictability. Subjects and objects that are routine and predictable (calendars, clocks, schedules, patterns) may hold extreme appeal. This is often because their neurological differences make it difficult for them to learn from experience, generalize, and read social cues, so much of life seems "random" to them. Predictable routines provide comfort and lessen anxiety.

Routines

Parents, care-givers, teachers, and employers can assist by providing routines when possible, preparing the individual prior to a change, and demonstrating understanding and providing assistance and practical supports when it is not possible or advisable to adhere to a comfortable routine.

Roadblocks

There was once a young man with autism who regularly went for a bike ride, following the same route each time. One day, when he did not return home on-time, his family found him standing at a sign indicating a road closure. His ASD made it difficult for him to imagine new responses or solutions to novel situations.

Many of us suffer from the same difficulty with "life's roadblocks." From receiving a diagnosis for a young child (whether or not it was anticipated), to facing difficult behaviors, to struggling through sleepless nights, to manipulating diets or medications to achieve maximum results, to striving to teach (or learn) an important but seemingly difficult lesson, to managing negative emotions such as fear, anxiety, and anger, we are frequently faced with what at first glance may appear to be the end of the road.

At such a roadblock, we need to determine whether we will shut down, or look for new options so that this becomes only a temporary setback. The key is to keep "putting one foot in front of the other!" At Social Incites, LLC, we say that this means continuing to take the next step to grow personally and interpersonally.

- Find just one thing to try that is different from what you have tried before.
- Allow yourself to rest for a moment, taking time to assess the situation and think through possible alternatives (but do not shut down)!
- Ask for directions. Utilize the creativity, gifts, and experiences of those around you to spark new possibilities for your situation.
- Remember that tomorrow is a new day, presenting new perspectives and opportunities to succeed.
- Look back at where you have been-- sometimes this perspective shows continued progress, even though it has been achieved through baby steps, or even when it feels as though you have not been moving at all!
- Recognize that the new route you take may end up being better in the long run than the one you were on previously!

The Social Response Pyramid™ can be helpful in providing understanding for a needed change in routine, as can other visuals and picture schedules. Sensory integration techniques can help individuals stay calm when change occurs.

ASD to Z

Our bodies are intended to function as "well-oiled machines," which receive input from our senses, and organize and process that information to respond effectively. Our senses include hearing, seeing, touching, tasting, and feeling, as well as the processes involving movement and gravity. When these systems are all working properly, and the brain is able to correctly interpret and respond to the information they send, we refer to this process as sensory integration; the senses are working together! However, when there are imperfections in this system, we call that *sensory processing disorder.*

Although there are many variations in the ways that sensory processing disorder can present itself, there are two main underlying problems. The first is when a person receives too much sensory input; in effect, their brain is overloaded. The second is when a person does not receive enough sensory input, resulting in a "craving" for sensory information.

Sensory processing disorder can affect the way a person responds to sound, touch, visual stimulation, movement, and other objects that they must interact with in their environment. It can make it difficult to focus on a conversation when there is other noise in the environment. It may also affect the individual's ability to make eye contact, if he or she is unable to use more than one sense at a time (i.e. looking and listening). Motor planning (the ability to get a person's body to do what he or she wants it to do in a coordinated manner) may also be adversely affected.

Sensory Integration Therapy, and a *sensory diet* of activities that address the unique needs of the individual can be extremely important in helping the individual with ASD to adapt to—and be successful in--his or her environment. Parents and care-givers can be trained to incorporate valuable activities and exercises in their daily routines to help meet the individual's unique sensory needs.

Some people need deep pressure in order to calm themselves and to help their brains organize and process sensory input. They may benefit from using a weighted vest, blanket, or wrist or ankle weights. There are many deep pressure activities that can be done with children. Swinging in a blanket, being rolled in a blanket like a "hot dog," pulling each other across the room in a laundry basket, and carrying heavy full plastic jugs are all excellent activities. The Wilbarger Brushing Method, developed by Patricia and Julia Wilbarger, uses a surgical scrub brush to stimulate the touch receptors, followed by deep pressure (proprioception) on the joints. A trained therapist could determine whether a child might benefit from brushing, and could instruct parents on how to use this and other sensory integration strategies with their child.

Although adults are generally able to control their environment by making decisions about the sights, smells, and sounds that surround them, as well as the activities that they engage in, children rarely have the "luxury" of avoiding uncomfortable sensory stimuli in this way. In a crowded, activity-filled classroom, there is often no opportunity to escape the noise and confusion. Activities such as finger painting, sculpting with clay, or dissecting a frog are planned for the entire class to participate in, and frequently, the student's performance is rated based on the successful completion of these tasks. It is important to talk with your child and his/her teacher to determine what activities and situations may be presenting challenges in the classroom and in other environments, and to help to provide a solution. There is much that can be done to help a child with sensory processing disorder!

Many fabulous resources are available on sensory integration. Be sure to check our web site at www.socialincites.com for recommendations. These resources help parents and professionals better understand the perspective of an individual who has difficulty with sensory integration, and provide helpful techniques for home and school.

ASD to Z

Teachers are in a unique position to promote success for all students.

An accurate understanding of ASD enables teachers to be compassionate role models for peers (both students and other school staff), and ensures that activities and expectations in the classroom accommodate both the strengths and challenges of the student with ASD. Frequent communication with parents and other professionals leads to creative problem-solving and helps to provide continuity across each of the student's environments.

A teacher increases the likelihood of calm, productive days in the classroom by approaching his or her tasks with flexibility, creativity, compassion, and a good sense of humor.

Remember that a "teacher" can be more than an instructor at the front of the classroom. Family members and friends are teachers of the *social curriculum.* They help individuals with ASD understand their environment, social expectations, nonverbal language, unspoken social rules, and a host of other concepts that may otherwise remain a "mystery" to those with ASD.

There are many people in the lives of individuals with ASD who also help teach valuable educational and life skills. The success of children, adolescents, and adults with ASD depends in large part on the cooperation and communication between each of these "coaches," whether they are professionals (teachers, doctors, therapists, counselors, psychologists, etc.), friends and family, or members of the community.

Remember that the opinions, experiences, and future responses of the children or adults in your home, classroom, workplace, etc. will be shaped and molded by YOU. Your attitudes, knowledge, experiences, reactions, etc. are somehow going to play a role in the success of friends, spouses, writers, teachers, political leaders, doctors, lawyers, garbage collectors, landlords, secretaries, scientists, parents, teachers, law enforcement professionals, cashiers, and more!

What a responsibility—and what an inspiration!

Social coaching and consulting and presentations can be accessed through Social Incites, LLC, and can be helpful to those supporting individuals with ASD.

How are you a teacher? What strategies do you use to be successful...and to help others to be successful?

_____

_____

_____

_____

_____

_____

_____

You are unique—an individual with value,
whether or not you have a diagnosis!

When a diagnosis is recent, the focus tends to be on the "symptoms" that led to the diagnosis, many of which are perceived as negatives. However, the diagnosis itself does not change a person; it only changes our basis of understanding the individual, and of relevant resources that could be helpful.

It is important to remember that an individual with ASD is first and foremost a PERSON, with a unique personality, and with feelings, fears, interests, and dreams. Keep those dreams alive and help to maintain the self-esteem of the person involved, through a positive outlook, and by promoting understanding with those who interact with that person in the home, school, workplace, and community.

People's needs change throughout their lives. This is certainly true of individuals with ASD. Since the diagnosis is only a part of who they are, it is also important to understand common issues related to various life stages, including toddlers, preschoolers, students in elementary, middle, and high school, college, the workplace and beyond...and to be aware of how those stages affect the unique needs of individuals with ASD. Regardless of the age of the individual, it is important that he or she has opportunities to participate successfully in social activities, and to contribute in meaningful ways.

Here is some of what I appreciate about people with autism:

1. **They have a unique perspective on life.** They see things I miss, they question things I take for granted, and they challenge

me to consider different ways of understanding life and those around me. My life is richer because of them.

2. **They have a more unbiased approach to people and situations.** I carry with me my own expectations, memories, and opinions, which cloud or direct the way I approach life. Their tendency to approach people and situations with a "clean slate," taking them at face value, is something that continues to have a positive influence on me.

3. **They contribute to my knowledge base.** Because of people with autism, I know more about trains, elevators, animals, dinosaurs, chickens, music, plants, sports statistics, computers, and video games than I ever would have otherwise. They have "broadened my horizons"—and our society has also benefited greatly from their interests and contributions!

4. **They require me to keep thinking and learning.** I have been interacting with people with autism spectrum disorders for over twenty years. I find that the more I know, the more I need to know. The need for flexibility, new approaches, novel ways to help them understand, and a better grasp on how they view the world drives me toward asking them more questions, reading more books, listening to more professionals in the field, talking to other parents and professionals, and trying new strategies. I recognize the tremendous value of this pursuit of understanding for both my personal and professional life.

5. **They make great friends!** I have numerous friends who are people with ASD. They are loyal, dependable, slow to judge or jump to conclusions, funny, and very knowledgeable. Because of them, I have also made wonderful friends who are teachers, parents, grandparents, employers, and others working to promote social insight and effectiveness all around the world.

Obviously, people with autism are not the only ones who are unique. Parents and other family members should ensure that they have activities and interests outside the responsibilities associated with meeting the needs of an individual with ASD. It is important that they evaluate their own unique abilities and challenges, set goals, and nurture other relationships.

Most of us could probably be accused of making mistakes with voice volume at one time or another. We may be too loud or too quiet for a given situation or environment. But some people, including those with ASD and other social cognitive challenges, frequently struggle to use the correct voice volume. Often they are not aware of how loud or quiet they are, or of how they affect people around them with their voice volume. Or they do not accurately "read" the expectations of others in any given environment to know how to adapt their voice volume to meet the expectations of others.

Some people may need to be taught specifically how and when to whisper, use a quiet "indoor voice," or speak more loudly. A combination of strategies is most likely to help them to be successful at meeting others' expectations:

1. **Sensory strategies:** People who have difficulties with sensory integration may perceive sounds differently than others. Some sounds may even be painful to them. It is important to consider what role sensory issues may play in a student's ability to perceive different sound levels and to respond effectively.

2. **Modeling:** Make sure you are personally using an effective voice volume for the given situation or environment. Raise awareness of the choices you make regarding voice volume, and help others through prompts and cues to do the same. Remember to affirm effective choices that they make!

3. **Role-play:** Take modeling one step further, where you and students take turns using different voice volumes, talking about the subtleties between them, how effective they are in a given situation or environment, how they affect other people, etc.

4. **Videotaping:** Videotape and then re-play a real-life situation or some of the modeling/role-playing mentioned previously. Discuss and analyze various aspects to give them opportunities to continue to learn about effective voice volume.
5. **Visuals** can be used to support learning and provide valuable cues to remind students which voice volume to use in a particular situation or environment:

Visual representations of this concept can be helpful. Working with the child, you can create a poster or 3-D model of a volume button or dial. Label it with different terms for a range of voice volume levels. As you discuss this concept, write examples of environments or situations where each is most likely to be appropriate. Practice saying a word or phrase in different volumes. Be sure to use those terms—and even the visual you have created-- consistently throughout your day!

Emotional regulation can also be difficult for people with ASD. They may react in an unexpected way (either too vehemently or with little or no response) to an event, environment, transition, person, sound, touch, or movement. They may find it difficult to calm themselves after what some term a *meltdown,* or they may get overwhelmed and *shut down.* They may need to be taught specific emotions (emotion vocabulary, and how each emotion looks or feels) so that they can identify those emotions in themselves and others, and begin to learn strategies for responding effectively to them.

Care-givers and others who interact regularly with individuals with ASD may also need assistance dealing with the variety of emotions that they experience. It is important to network with others, to celebrate successes, and to receive encouragement and support along the way.

The *Social Response Pyramid™* can help plan strategies for avoiding often-unproductive *authentic responses,* and instead producing *socially effective responses.*

Often, we view the words and actions of people with ASD as meaningless, unanticipated, inappropriate, or even defiant. Yet they usually have very valid reasons for their responses! *Why do they do what they do?* Here are some possible explanations, some of which are a review of topics already covered in this booklet:

1. Sensory processing. Each of us is constantly bombarded by sensory information. What our brains do with that information can vary widely, and can produce just as wide a variety of responses!

2. Being motivated by special interests. People may ignore or refuse other topics or activities, not to be rude or disobedient, but because they are more interested in --or feel compelled to follow--opportunities to pursue or engage in their special interest.

3. Inability to glean from external assistance, including learning from past experience, establishing a connection between rewards, consequences, and their behavior, or to ask for help from others.

4. Misinterpretation of language or the social environment, including interpreting things literally, missing intended meanings, overlooking or misunderstanding social expectations, and incorrectly processing what they hear or see. A lack of information or experience may also make it difficult to anticipate how others will respond, or to communicate how a person is feeling or what he or she is thinking.

5. Unique personality traits and characteristics of age and maturity level. Sometimes people "do what they do" because they are young and inexperienced, or because they are more extroverted or introverted. Many of the behaviors observed in individuals with ASD cannot--and should not--be attributed to their diagnosis. Sometimes they (and we) will make an inappropriate choice, or an immature decision, or take an uncalculated risk.

If we keep an open mind, and make a true effort to understand why those around us do what they do, we can become more compassionate and effective in our interactions with others!

marks the spot

Strive for an accurate understanding of each individual's interests, abilities, challenges, and goals.

Since these characteristics change over time, this process should be done periodically, through input from the individual, as well as parents, professionals, and others who are familiar with him or her. Formal testing may be valuable, along with informal observations.

Personal journals, doctor's reports, school report cards, and workplace employee evaluations may become an important gauge of daily successes or overall progress, and help to identify strategies that work, and new goals to achieve.

As students get older, they can begin to participate more fully in IEPs, doctor's appointments, therapy sessions, and more, for practice in discussing their abilities and needs, and learning to advocate for themselves. Older individuals may benefit from a *personal success plan,* (available through Social Incites' coaching and consulting services), or a *PCP* (*Person Centered Planning*) session. Being actively involved can help people with ASD develop a vested interest in their personal responsibilities and success.

ASD to Z

Look how far you have come!

Over time, whether you have just recently learned about ASD (maybe by reading this booklet) or have been walking this road for many years, you have likely increased your personal understanding of ASD. You may have had the opportunity to educate others or to network with them. The individual on whose behalf you are working has likely made identifiable improvement in one area or another—or perhaps in several!

Find ways to celebrate benchmarks and progress, and to set realistic goals for the future! It may be advantageous to keep a personal journal, copies of past IEP's, photos, and a collection of scripts or plans ("Social Incites") written for the individual over the years. These help to gain perspective regarding the progress that everyone has made, even when it seems as though it is accomplished through one tiny step at a time.

Social Incites, LLC has a variety of resources available for understanding autism across the lifespan. During toddlerhood, parents may need help dealing with toileting and tantrums, as well as teaching basic communication and interaction skills. Adolescence can be a particularly difficult time, as many individuals have an increased awareness of their differences and difficulty "fitting in" socially. Depression is not uncommon. Adulthood also brings unique challenges, as peers may not be aware of the diagnosis, or may not be particularly understanding or supportive. It is important that people learn to advocate for themselves, and that they continue to learn strategies for identifying and meeting the expectations of others.

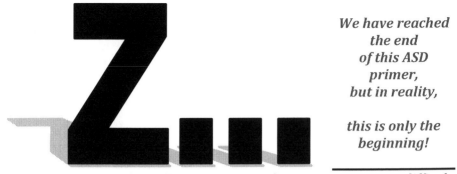

We have reached the end of this ASD primer, but in reality,

this is only the beginning!

New research will continue to bring answers to difficult questions, innovative and dedicated people will persist in developing new tools to foster learning and successful interactions, and will continue to form partnerships with others to meet the needs of their children, students, spouses, employees/employers, and friends with ASD.

Individuals with ASD, with the support and encouragement of the people who interact with them, will continue to enhance the lives of those around them through their unique approach to life.

Together, we will build a world where differences are not only accepted, but celebrated, where the strengths and unique characteristics of people with ASD are seen as beautiful fibers in the tapestry of our lives, and where we eagerly seek out, acknowledge, and appreciate their contributions to our families, classrooms, workplaces, and communities.

Dear Readers,

I am aware that as people hear a diagnosis of an autism spectrum disorder (ASD) applied to a loved one (or themselves) for the first time, they may feel that they are being launched into a long and uncertain journey.

Fortunately, our understanding of ASD—and the impact that it has on those with the diagnosis, as well as the people who interact with them—has changed considerably in recent years. In the past, news media and available resources detailed the negatives of ASD and the grim prognosis for these individuals. Now, however, people are able to access helpful resources, including books, web sites, and professionals in the field, as well as others who share similar experiences. Research has indicated that the prognosis can be excellent, especially when early intervention enables children to benefit from a wide variety of strategies to meet their needs and enhance their abilities, although a person is never too old to benefit from appropriate interventions.

My goal in writing this resource is that those who read it will receive valuable information, support, and hope. The intent is that this booklet would be your starting point as you begin to investigate the diagnosis and to gather resources and direction for your journey. Most importantly, I hope that this booklet will inspire you to celebrate the uniqueness of individuals with ASD, and to value your role in promoting social understanding and social effectiveness as you travel this road with them.

Over the years, this resource (revised and expanded with this fourth edition) has provided valuable information and support to over 20,000 people around the world, many of whom have been given this booklet free of charge as families new to the diagnosis!

We hope this book will provide an opportunity for you to educate or support friends, family, and other community members. If you would like to order additional copies of this booklet to give away, or would like to recommend it to someone else, please go to www.socialincites.com.

Your support of Social Incites, LLC enables us to provide this resource to people new to the diagnosis, as part of our mission of providing insights to incite people to grow personally and interpersonally.

Thank you for partnering with us in this important work!

Laurel A. Falvo, CFLE, CETS
Certified Family Life Educator
Certified Employment Training Specialist
President, Social Incites, LLC

PEOPLE with AUTISM: Why Do They Do What They Do?

"Try to understand why people do what they do.
They have their reasons
even if we don't know what they are."

Have you ever thought about that with respect to individuals with autism spectrum disorders (ASD)? Often we are quick to view their comments, silences, meltdowns, and actions as meaningless, unanticipated, inappropriate, or even defiant. Yet if or when they are able to process and to voice explanations for their actions, they usually have very valid reasons for them!

What then causes them to do what they do? Here are some possible explanations:

1. Sensory processing. Each of us is constantly bombarded by sensory information. What our brains do with that information can vary widely, and can produce just as wide a variety of responses! But frequently those responses are perfectly valid given the way that our brains processed the input. Do you perceive a noise as painful? It makes sense that you would cover your ears, run from the noise, or try to drown it out in another manner. Are you adverse to certain sensations? Then it seems appropriate that you would avoid getting your hands dirty (and any tasks that would lead in that direction), or refuse to wear particular clothing, or react abruptly (or even forcefully) to distasteful touch. These responses make even more sense when paired with some of the following explanations.

2. Being motivated by special interests. Individuals with ASD typically have an area (or areas) of intense interest, to the exclusion of others. They may ignore or refuse other topics or activities, not to be rude or disobedient, but because they are more interested in --or feel compelled to follow--opportunities to pursue or engage in their special interest.

3. Inability to glean from external assistance. The nature of their diagnosis makes it difficult for individuals with ASD to learn

ASD to Z

from past experience, to establish a connection between rewards, consequences, and their behavior, or to ask for help from others.

4. Misinterpretation of language or the social environment. ASD often causes individuals to interpret things literally, to miss intended meanings, to overlook or misunderstand social expectations, and to incorrectly process what they hear (auditory processing), see, or experience. Their lack of information or experience may also make it difficult for them to anticipate how others will respond, or to communicate how they are feeling or what they are thinking.

5. Unique personality traits and characteristics of their age and maturity level. Sometimes people "do what they do" because they are young and inexperienced, or because their personality dictates that they are more extroverted or introverted. Many of the behaviors that we observe in individuals with ASD cannot--and should not--be attributed to their diagnosis. Sometimes they may make an inappropriate choice, or an immature decision, or take an uncalculated risk, just because they're human. Let's face it--haven't we all "been there, done that" many times over?

If we keep an open mind, and make a true effort to understand why those around us do what they do, we will make great strides in our efforts at promoting social effectiveness. "When we try to understand why people do what they do, we have more compassion." What a great goal--to become more compassionate parents, teachers, administrators, employers, therapists, doctors, neighbors, and friends through our efforts to better understand ourselves and others!

Laurel A. Falvo, CFLE, CETS
Certified Family Life Educator
Certified Employment Training Specialist
President, Social Incites, LLC
www.socialincites.com

About the Illustrator

Vincente Rangel, a husband, and father of four sons, is a versatile artist who brings to life people, landscapes, objects, and more! He uses pencil sketches, acrylics, and watercolors, and does well with all of them. He has produced political cartoons, artwork for businesses (including window displays), and now is collaborating on various resources with Social Incites, LLC. We're amazed at how quickly he can produce new illustrations for us, capturing the essence of "social"--and whatever other goals we're trying to achieve! If you are interested in having Vincente create illustrations or paintings for you, please contact us.

Coaching and Consulting

Laurel has combined her years of professional and parenting experience, along with her training as an elementary teacher and Certified Family Life Educator and a Certified Employment Training Specialist, to provide **Coaching and Consulting** services. Parents, teachers, young adults, and children from around the world use her "social coaching" services to identify goals and develop strategies for improving their lives and enjoying social effectiveness. She and her husband Steve also provide "rehabilitation services" such as **job development and employment coaching** benefiting both employers and employees. More information is available at www.socialincites.com.

Social Incites™ Newsletter & Blog

 Social Incites™ is a weekly email article/blog written by Laurel Falvo to promote personal and interpersonal growth and autism awareness. People can subscribe to this free resource and read past issues at www.socialincites.com.

The Social Response Pyramid(TM)

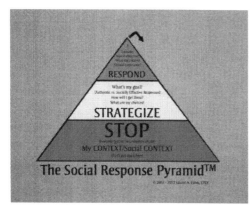

This educational tool, developed by Laurel Falvo, is a visual representation of social understanding and social effectiveness--how we can better understand ourselves and others (including people with autism spectrum disorders) in order to develop and utilize strategies to increase the effectiveness of our responses. It can be used by anyone and for anyone! More information and supports can be found at www.socialincites.com.

Presentations

Laurel Falvo is available to provide trainings on *The Social Response Pyramid*™ and a variety of other topics, either in person or via phone or Skype. Each presentation is geared to the unique needs of the given audience. Topics include parenting, autism, inclusion, successful employment, tools for success, and more. More information can be found on our web site.

Storytelling

Steve Falvo, Laurel's husband, enjoys telling stories that illustrate social interactions and the lessons that can be learned from them. His stories are both educational and enjoyable. Some are now available in book form, including *The Pick-A-Roo!* and *Kidnapped...in the Erie Islands!* Both can be found on our web site.

Hand in Hand:

A Story about Asperger Syndrome...
and a Very Significant Friendship

By Laurel A. Falvo

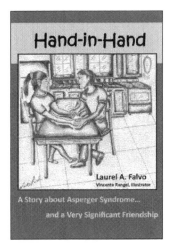

Join Rory Hollander and his cousin Alyssa as they navigate one week of their final year of high school, appreciating their unique friendship even while acknowledging the ways it will change in the near future.

Asperger Syndrome, mutual understanding, helpful strategies, and respect are just part of this busy time in their lives, along with both positive and negative relationships, college plans, job prospects, and creative writing assignments.

Regardless of your age or related experience, as you hear their story, and use the enclosed discussion guide, you're likely to increase your understanding and appreciation for people with Asperger Syndrome and other forms of autism, and add to your toolbox of strategies to help yourself and others experience social success.

Hopefully, like both Rory and Alyssa, you'll be inspired to make a difference in your own corner of the world!

(This book is available at www.socialincites.com).

Made in the USA
Charleston, SC
10 March 2014